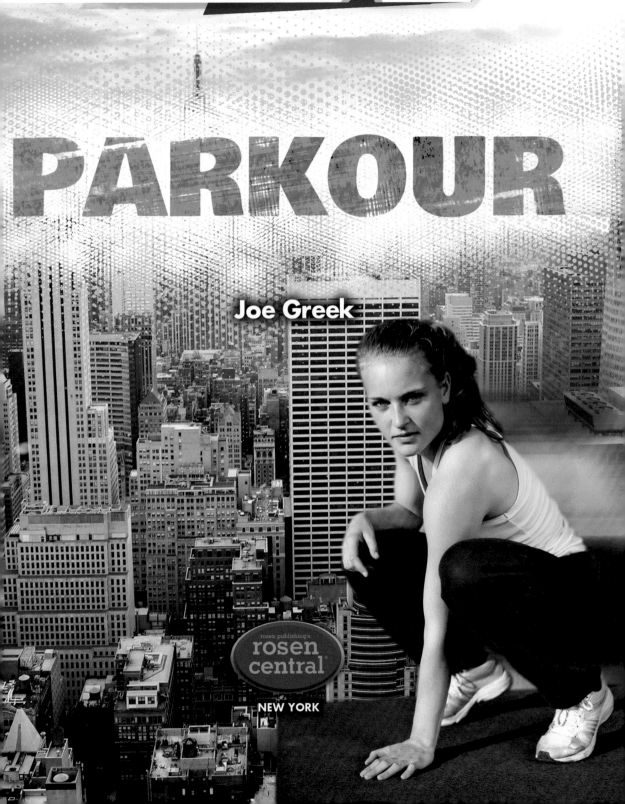

SPORTS **TO THE E** TREME™

PARKOUR

Joe Greek

rosen publishing's
rosen central®

NEW YORK

Published in 2016 by The Rosen Publishing Group, Inc.
29 East 21st Street, New York, NY 10010

First Edition

Library of Congress Cataloging-in-Publication Data

Greek, Joe.
Parkour/Joe Greek.
    pages cm.—(Sports to the extreme)
Includes bibliographical references and index.
ISBN 978-1-4994-3553-5 (library bound)—ISBN 978-1-4994-3555-9 (pbk.)—
ISBN 978-1-4994-3556-6 (6-pack)
1. Running—Juvenile literature. 2. Parkour—Juvenile literature. 3. Extreme sports—Juvenile literature. I. Title.
GV1061.G675 2016
796.42—dc23

                                                     2014045494

Manufactured in the United States of America

CONTENTS

INTRODUCTION

You've probably seen videos of young men and women leaping across rooftops, climbing brick walls, and doing backflips off park benches. Known as parkour, kids and adults across the world have become fascinated with this popular method of physical fitness and training. It has become so popular in recent years that there's even a good chance that you or your friends are already practicing parkour at the playground or park.

To many, parkour may not look like a serious physical fitness discipline. However, enthusiasts believe that parkour can be as beneficial as other disciplines like yoga and karate. Parkour is more than just jumping and doing backflips. The basic definition of parkour is getting from point A to point B as efficiently and quickly as possible. This involves both physical and mental discipline. People who train in parkour often do so in order to improve their health. Others take up the practice to improve their confidence to overcome obstacles in and out of training.

Parkour is community driven, and perhaps nothing has shaped it more than the online community. Modern parkour has quickly evolved over the past few decades. Much of the change, as well as the sport's increasing popularity, has come as a result of the Internet. Enthusiasts of parkour use the

With a good grip and quick movement, ordinary surroundings turn into parkour obstacles.

Internet to share videos, techniques, and tips with one another. The ability to easily connect and share with other enthusiasts has helped keep the momentum behind the sport going strong.

In the following sections, we will discuss the origins of parkour and the people who revolutionized it. You'll find out how parkour has become a part of our culture that can be seen throughout movies and even video games. Finally, we will cover the basics of the discipline and the moves that professional parkour athletes build their styles upon.

CHAPTER ONE

HISTORY AND PHILOSOPHY OF PARKOUR

The story behind parkour is almost as unpredictable as the practice itself. Parkour can be considered a type of physical fitness practice. At the same time, it can also be considered a sport. It focuses on self-improvement of the individual, but it is also community and location driven. Though parkour has become well-known only in the past several years, it has been evolving for more than a century.

"TO BE STRONG TO BE USEFUL"

At the beginning of the twenti-eth century, French naval officer Georges Hébert was stationed on the Caribbean island of Martinique. A dangerous volcanic eruption in 1902 threatened to wipe out an entire village. Springing to action,

Many of the techniques found in the Natural Method can still be seen in modern-day parkour.

6

Hébert helped almost seven hundred villagers escape to safety. The event led Hébert to strongly believe that physical strength, courage, and selflessness were important qualities for an individual to be valuable in his or her community. Eventually, this belief became the basis for his motto, "Être fort pour être utile," which means, "To be strong to be useful."

While traveling the world, Hébert was also inspired by the physical strength and agility of indigenous people. Living in often-harsh environments, such as jungles, indigenous peoples seemed to be masters at moving through challenging surroundings.

After returning to France, Hébert began teaching physical fitness at the University of Reims. It was during this time that he created his own new style of physical training, known as the Natural Method, which included swimming, running, jumping, climbing, throwing, lifting, balancing, and self-defense. Hébert saw no need for competition in his training. He believed that it would only distract from the psychological goal of encouraging selflessness.

Natural Method training took place outdoors. Students were forced to maneuver through the natural environment. Hébert also developed a series of drills and equipment that the students had to use in their practice. Often referred to as the Grandfather of Parkour, Hébert's physical fitness routines became known as the *parcours du combattant*, meaning "obstacle course."

OVERCOMING THE OBSTACLES

Between World War I and World War II, Hébert's teachings continued to gain a following. The Natural Method, and the use of Hébert's obstacles in particular, were even used by the French military to train soldiers.

Obstacle courses are generally a series of natural or man-made obstacles that an individual or team navigates through. An obstacle course may include barriers, such as climbing walls, pools of water

The obstacle course is an important part of military training. It is used to test and build a soldier's mental and physical strength.

to swim across, and low wires to crawl under. Athletes who go through obstacle courses use their minds to figure out the best way to overcome different challenges in their path.

Today, most militaries around the world use obstacle courses to prepare soldiers for the different environments and situations they may face. Many schools also use obstacle courses as a part of their physical education programs. Obstacle courses are often considered the inspiration behind public fitness trails as well.

RISE OF MODERN PARKOUR

Raymond Belle was born to French parents in Vietnam in 1939. He later became orphaned as a result of the wars that affected Vietnam. Under the protection of the French army, he was trained in military survival and aspects of the Natural Method at a young age.

Belle used his military training to experiment with different techniques to escape captivity and dangerous situations that could occur in wartime Vietnam. Belle's freestyle training techniques became known as parkour. Eventually, he was able to move to France, where he joined the Paris Fire Brigade. Throughout his career, he became respected for his athletic ability and courage. A role model to many children in France, his son David would follow in his footsteps and use parkour for physical training.

Born in 1973, David Belle was trained in parkour by his dad at a young age. His dad taught him much of his physical training through games. David enjoyed pushing himself to overcome obstacles and to not let anything get in his way. In his youth, he also practiced gymnastics and track and field. He pre-ferred to practice his training outside in the woods, where he could use obstacles such as fallen trees.

In the mid-1980s, the Belles moved to Lisses, France. It was in Lisses that David began to redefine the parkour training techniques he had learned from his father. At the center of the town was a park that had several large works of art, such as sculptures. Visualizing the pieces of art as obstacles, David was soon sprinting, jumping, and swinging on and off of them. This may sound like every-day horseplay to most people. However, David had taken elements of his father's style of parkour and obstacle training out of nature and placed them in an urban environment.

David Belle began training and developing parkour at an early age. Today, he works as a stunt coordinator and movie star.

As a teenager, David's urban parkour became popular among his group of friends. Together, in 1997, David and his friends created the first professional parkour group, which was called the Yamakasi.

Following in his dad's footsteps, David joined the French military and also became a firefighter. David's career in the military, however, did not last long. David eventually left the strict life of the military to dedicate his time to parkour. For several years, David worked odd jobs as a warehouse worker and a security guard. At one point,

THE YAMAKASI

In 1997, the first professional parkour group was founded in France by David Belle, Sébastien Foucan, Yann Hnautra, Charles Perrière, Malik Diouf, Guylain N'Guba-Boyeke, Châu Belle-Dinh, and Williams Belle. Called the Yamakasi, the name is often mistaken as having a Japanese meaning. The name actually means "strong spirit" in the Lingala language, which is spoken in the Democratic Republic of the Congo.

The Yamakasi was the first group to organize gatherings at which people practiced parkour. The members were instrumental in helping to popularize and train others in practicing parkour. Members of the group were featured in the French films *Yamakasi* (2001) and *Les fils du vent* (2004). The most notable members, David Belle and Sébastien Foucan, both left the group, which still maintains a following today.

David was able to spend time in India, where he trained in the martial art of kung fu.

A video by David, called *Air Speed Man*, became popular on the Internet in the late 1990s. In it, clips highlight David leaping from high ledges, effortlessly running up a climbing wall, and performing backflips from dangerous heights. People around the world wanted to be able to pull off the same physical stunts as David. Soon, David was hired to perform in movies and television, and his style of parkour picked up a devoted following of students.

PHILOSOPHY: BREAKING DOWN BARRIERS

In French, male students of parkour are known as *traceurs* while female students are referred to as *traceuses*. In general, though, *traceur* is the accepted term. All serious students of parkour share a similar philosophy behind the training. Simply put, parkour is about overcoming obstacles by using the body to get from point A to point B as quickly and efficiently as possible.

Similar to the Natural Method, students practice parkour in order to develop both physically and mentally. People often face obstacles in life that they believe they are either physically or mentally unable to overcome. The philosophy of parkour, however, suggests that most obstacles can be overcome with practice.

If the average person is running toward a tree, he or she will immediately stop before running into it. A traceur, though, may set a goal of reaching a certain branch on the tree before moving past it. The traceur might jump and grab onto one branch and start climbing the tree to his or her intended target. Our minds often try to protect us from physical dangers by making us feel scared or uneasy. These mental obstacles are what the philosophy of parkour tries to knock down. By practicing different parkour moves and attempting to overcome physical challenges over and over, the mental obstacles disappear. Eventually, students can find themselves running through the world with a new courage and the confidence to overcome obstacles in all parts of their lives.

"Parkour is such a broad thing. People try and put a definition on it. But we like it to be broad because it can be anything to anybody," said traceur Daniel Arroyo in an article on ESPN.com. "It's physical obstacles—it's a discipline and an art; by definition it's getting from A to B as fast as possible. But it helps you overcome things mentally. It's self-therapy for me. But for someone else, it could just be physical enjoyment."

A CREATIVE ART FORM

Similar to the Natural Method, the motivation behind parkour is generally considered to be one of self-improvement. Unlike most sports and physical fitness programs, parkour does not have a set of defined rules. How parkour is practiced is simply up to the individual.

For students to gain the most out of parkour, they will need to develop their own routines. Because of this lack of structure, parkour allows individuals to be as creative as they want. What works for some people may not be the best practice for others in parkour.

Training in parkour can incorporate other interests into a routine. Some people even include skateboards in their training routines. For two or more people that are training together, a routine can be turned into a game. For example, a group can turn a game of tag into an exciting parkour training routine. In this instance, one individual is "it" and the others have to copy that person's moves until someone else is tagged and becomes the new "it."

A parkour enthusiast will not master difficult moves overnight. Frequent practice helps individuals perfect challenging moves and develop personal techniques.

TO COMPETE OR NOT TO COMPETE

Hébert taught his students to avoid being competitive with one another when training in the Natural Method. Many students and teachers of parkour also speak strongly against competition. To some, competition is simply another obstacle that should be overcome.

Parkour enthusiasts are divided on whether or not competition is a good thing for the community. There are many arguments for and many against competition. On the side that opposes competition, these people believe that it can lead to an unhealthy obsession with being victorious. The opposition also believes that competitions can lead to parkour becoming exploited by companies that want to make money off of it.

WORLD FREERUNNING & PARKOUR FEDERATION

The World Freerunning & Parkour Federation, or WFPF, is one of the premier organizations dedicated to the practice of parkour. Founded in 2007 by Ryan Doyle, the WFPF is dedicated to promoting the philosophy and practice of parkour. With members around the world, the WFPF offers parkour training certification programs to individuals who want to become teachers of the discipline.

In 2010, MTV partnered with the WFPF to air the television show *Ultimate Parkour Challenge*. The show, which featured competition among members of the WFPF, was the subject of much debate within the parkour community.

On the other hand, supporters of competition believe that it could only help to spread parkour to new audiences. Another argument is that friendly competitions can encourage people to strive harder in their training. Nonetheless, there is always room for both groups to enjoy parkour in their own ways.

COMMUNITY SPIRIT

In the years since David Belle and members of the Yamakasi became well-known, parkour has become incredibly popular. So popular, in fact, that parkour has grown from an underground practice into a discipline known worldwide. Parkour can easily be mistaken for being a purely individual sport or training discipline. After all, it tends to be focused on the self-improvement of the individual. However, the practice is actually quite community centric.

Part of the philosophy behind parkour is to be selfless and useful to the community, as Hébert promoted through the Natural Method. The idea of selflessness and contributing to the community was not lost with the early leaders of parkour either. The parkour community can be found in the real world and online.

Thanks to an open and supportive community of enthusiasts, new parkour techniques and moves are continually being shared.

Students and teachers often share their techniques with each other online through blogs, forums, and videos. In this way, more people are able to learn how to improve their own routines. Many groups and clubs now exist across the world.

Periodically, gatherings known as jams are held for parkour enthusiasts. At jams, enthusiasts meet up to train together and display their abilities. Jams are often hosted by parkour clubs and are open to the public. Jams are a great way for newcomers to the practice to learn from veteran traceurs.

CHAPTER TWO

A GLOBAL MOVEMENT

Parkour has greatly evolved since its origins in the Natural Method. For much of the past century, though, the Natural Method and parkour were generally unknown. It wasn't until the early 2000s that parkour began to show signs of growing popularity.

In the past decade, parkour has become a growing fad around the world. In the streets of New York City, Tokyo, and New Delhi, traceurs can be found running and jumping. Enthusiasts of parkour come from all ages and backgrounds. They share a common interest, however, which usually involves self-improvement while having fun at the same time.

GOING VIRAL ONLINE

In 2003, the documentary *Jump London* was aired in England.

Parkour can be found almost anywhere. These athletes are showing their moves in Hong Kong, China.

19

film follows traceurs Sébastien Foucan, Jérôme Ben Aoues, and Johann Vigroux as they run around the English capital. Showcasing daring parkour moves at famous landmarks, such as Royal Albert Hall, the stars also discuss the philosophy and purpose of their movements. Up until the release of *Jump London*, parkour had remained fairly unknown to most people. The documentary quickly became popular in England. Its success even led to the sequel *Jump Britain*, which was aired in 2005.

The *Jump* films helped to raise awareness of parkour, inspiring new enthusiasts. At the same time, websites like YouTube had also recently become popular. Video-sharing websites offered a new space for people to show their interests to the world. In no time, traceurs were using the Internet to demonstrate their skills to a global audience. Amateur and professional parkour videos (such as Belle's *Air Speed Man*) were being watched around the world. Many went viral by gaining millions of views and being shared around the Internet.

Many viral parkour videos show off the incredible moves of traceurs. However, there are also videos that become viral because they show people making mistakes or even getting seriously injured. A video of traceur Matt Quinlan from New Zealand failing to make a proper landing went viral in 2014. After falling short in a jump, Quinlan hit a shipping container face-first and broke a tooth. Videos, such as Quinlan's, in which people are injured while doing parkour should not be viewed

Parkour's popularity has resulted in a flood of online videos that range from homemade clips to professionally filmed training videos.

for entertainment. They should be seen as a reminder of the dangerous side of parkour.

Since the mid-2000s, parkour has continued to be a popular topic online. For example, a search on YouTube for the term "parkour" generates more than six million results. The Internet has provided enthusiasts and the curious with a quick way to share, learn, and even participate. There are countless discussion forums dedicated to parkour that range from those where people express general enthusiasm about the practice to those for fans of local traceurs. Blogs are great resources for traceurs who enjoy learning about the techniques of other traceurs. Social networks, such as Facebook, also make it easy for traceurs to plan jams.

SÉBASTIEN FOUCAN

Born in France in 1974, Sébastien Foucan was an early pioneer in the world of parkour and is considered the founder of freerunning. He grew up in Lisses, France, where he met parkour founder David Belle. With Belle and others, Foucan founded the Yamakasi group. He joined the military and worked as a firefighter in Paris for three years. From the recognition he gained from the 2003 documentary *Jump London*, Foucan found relative success as an actor. Madonna used Foucan in her 2005 video for the song "Jump," and he joined her onstage during her 2006 tour. Today, he teaches freerunning classes and does public speaking events.

FREERUNNING

The practice of parkour has now itself led to the creation of another training method. In the documentary *Jump London*, Foucan used the term "freerunning" to describe parkour to English-speaking audiences. Eventually, though, "freerunning" came to describe Foucan's particular style of parkour. In freerunning, parkour incorporates techniques from different athletic styles, including acrobatics, gymnastics, and capoeira. The main philosophy behind freerunning is to be creative and do what feels best.

"Freerunning is the art of expressing yourself in your environment without limitations: it is the art of movement and action," Foucan says in his book *Freerunning: Find Your Way*. "For me, action is the most important thing in life. People who 'do' live their lives to the full; the rest just talk about it. My way is not about performing—it is simply the physical expression of being at one with your body and your mind."

The difference between traditional parkour and freerunning is the purpose behind the movements. In parkour, traceurs are focused on getting from point A to point B as efficiently and quickly as possible. In freerunning, on the other hand, creativity takes center stage. David Belle has said that parkour is purpose driven. Belle was quoted in a 2007 article in the *New Yorker* stating that parkour is "a very different mind-set from just doing things to look good."

Freerunning, which uses more daring moves than traditional parkour, has gained a large following as well. Focusing more on showing off moves

Enthusiasts are often divided on what the difference between parkour and freerunning really is.

than on getting from point A to point B, freerunning can be very dangerous. In 2013, Russian freerunner Pavel Kashin attempted a backflip on a ledge sixteen stories high. Kashin lost his balance after making the landing and fell over the ledge to his death. Stories like Kashin's are not unheard of in the freerunning and parkour communities.

THE TRACEURS OF HOLLYWOOD AND VIDEO GAMES

In 2006, Sébastien Foucan was cast to play the role of Mollaka in the film *Casino Royale*. The film, which is part of the James Bond series, begins with an epic chase scene. Foucan's character is chased through a construction site by James Bond (played by Daniel Craig). For nearly seven minutes, the two characters' exciting string of leaps, rolls, and climbing amazed audiences. *Casino Royale* marked the first time that parkour had been used in a blockbuster film.

Traceurs, like Foucan and David Belle, have frequently been hired to perform in movies and television over the past decade. *Brick Mansion* (2014), *Live Free or Die Hard* (2007), and *Sherlock Holmes: A Game of Shadows* (2011) are just a few of the major films to use parkour and traceurs. Viewers sometimes don't realize that the parkour movements in the movies are actually performed by real people. The skills of professional traceurs, such as Foucan and Belle, can puzzle audiences that are not familiar with parkour.

Parkour has not been limited to just movies, though. Video game makers have also found inspiration in the freestyle movements of traceurs. In 2007, the award-winning game *Assassin's Creed* was released on several video game systems. The makers of *Assassin's Creed* based many of the movements performed by the game's main

Sébastien Foucan's unforgettable performance in *Casino Royale* propelled parkour into the international spotlight.

character on those of traceurs. The success of the video game has led to the release of several sequels. Several other video games have also used parkour movements, including games in the *Prince of Persia* and *Sonic the Hedgehog* series.

PARKOUR IN THE BATTLEFIELD

For decades, militaries around the world have used obstacle courses as a part of their training. While obstacles are a large part of parkour, there are other parts of the practice that are now starting to become used in military training. Certain aspects of parkour make it great training for modern warfare. Unlike Hébert's Natural Method training, which generally took place in nature, parkour is geared more toward street environments. In recent wars in Afghanistan and Iraq, battles were often fought in cities.

In the past few years, the British Royal Marines (BRM) have enlisted the help of professional traceurs to train troops in parkour. The trainers teach marines parkour moves, like the kong vault, running cat, and crane, to help them improve their combat skills in urban environments. Two of the techniques the BRM found useful are the ability to jump from roof to roof and to drop from heights. In urban environments, marines can use parkour to move with speed and agility during intense street battles.

"We found some of the moves were relevant for battle," Captain Sean Lerwill told the *Guardian* in 2008. "For them (traceurs) it is about artistic expression. For example, they will run along a wall keeping a low profile because it looks good, but we need to do the same thing in urban combat to stay safe."

Parkour has not yet gained widespread adoption by militaries. To some people, parkour is viewed as being "counterculture," which means disrespecting authority or rebelling against society. Because of this view, parkour is not often viewed as being serious. "I expected to find people who were a little bit lazy and maybe even involved in drug culture," Lerwill said. "But they were nothing like that." According to the article in the *Guardian*, when the parkour trainers visited a BRM obstacle course, they completed it within the time needed to qualify as a marine. One day, parkour training could become required among troops as its benefits are more understood.

PARKOUR AROUND THE WORLD

Parkour has spread like wildfire throughout the world. Fueled by shared videos on the Internet, parkour has moved beyond Europe and the United States to countries you might least expect it to thrive in.

In the Middle Eastern country of Iran, a group of young women made headlines for embracing parkour. In many countries, it would not be surprising to see a woman training in parkour. Iran, however, is known for being very conservative. By law, women must wear a head-piece, known as a hijab, that covers their hair. Additionally, women in Iran have to wear loose clothing that does not reveal the shape of their bodies. The women in Iran that train in parkour face the disapproval of some in their communities. However, many of these women see parkour as a way to relieve stress and become stronger individuals. "There was a jump I couldn't do at first ... learning it made me realize I am capable of doing anything and defeating any obstacle," a 2014 article by the *Daily News* quotes Sedighian Rad as saying. "I feel free."

In the Gaza Strip, parkour has become a way for many youths to escape the conflict in that region. After seeing the *Jump London* documentary, a group of Palestinian youths founded the Gaza Parkour Team in 2005. "It makes them feel freedom in their souls, despite the many restrictions of living in Gaza—the blockade, the occupation, unemployment, the lack of places to have fun. They have so much fun with parkour," group founder Abdullah Anshasi told the Italian magazine *Domus* in 2013.

PUSH FOR THE OLYMPICS

In 2014, members of the professional parkour community, including Dan Edwardes of Parkour Generation, met with the International Olympics Committee (IOC). The purpose of the meeting was to discuss the possibility of including parkour in the global competitions. Many traceurs believe that competitions like the Olympics go against the principles of parkour. However, there are other traceurs and enthusiasts who believe that competitive parkour events will not have a negative impact on those who wish to pursue the practice noncompetitively. "There are tens of millions of people who run, who don't do it competitively," Edwardes said in an interview with National Public Radio. "So running as a discipline isn't necessarily competitive, but it does have a competitive element to it."

MAJOR COMPETITIONS AND GATHERINGS

The original philosophy behind parkour was against competitions, but that has not prevented parkour-related events from occurring. In fact, there have been numerous freerunning competitions in recent years. Competitions take place on both local and international stages. Parkour

Gatherings provide parkour and freerunning enthusiasts with a common ground to demonstrate their moves and engage in friendly competition.

and freerunning websites and forums are often the best places to find out about planned competitions.

One of the most popular freerunning competitions is the Red Bull Art of Motion. This event brings professional freerunning athletes together to showcase and compete against one another. The competition began in 2007 and has occurred every year since, with the exception of 2008. Participants are scored by technique, execution, fluidity, creativity, and style. On October 4, 2014, the competition was held on the Greek island of Santorini for the fourth year in a row. Out of eighteen professional freerunners, nineteen-year-old Dimitris Kyrsanidis from Thessaloniki, Greece, took home first place.

Competitions for teams are also held. In 2011, G4TV hosted the Jump City: Seattle competition. Filmed and aired on television, the competition pitted four American parkour and freerunning teams against each other. Team Tempest, a well-known group from Los Angeles, took first place.

CHAPTER THREE

PARKOUR IN ACTION

Watching videos of traceurs and actually doing parkour are two different things. The fluidity of traceurs' movements often makes parkour and freerunning look easy to do. However, professional traceurs usually have years of experience and training.

Like any serious athlete, a professional traceur has to have dedication to the discipline. Traceurs practice parkour frequently in order to stay in good physical shape. Additionally, they have to take care of their bodies in order to avoid getting hurt.

GEARING UP

Parkour requires much less money to get into than most other sports and fitness training programs do. Parkour does not require a gym membership or expert trainer. It also doesn't require special clothing or protective padding.

The main item of clothing that a traceur needs is a good pair of sneakers. With all the running and jumping, it's important for traceurs to provide comfort to their feet. Traceurs have to be flexible as they move around. Blue jeans and other restrictive

Traceurs have to be flexible and quick in their movements. Comfortable and not-too-tight clothing is a necessity for anyone practicing parkour.

pants are not a good idea for training. A pair of jogging pants with a drawstring to make them tight around the waist is a good investment. Any T-shirt will be suitable for a parkour training session.

There are many websites and organizations online that claim to sell the "best" or "official" equipment and clothing of parkour. Don't be fooled by such claims. Traceurs should dress comfortably and not worry about being stylish. Remember, it's not the clothes that make the athlete.

PARKOUR TRAINING FACILITIES AND COACHES

In recent years, the rising popularity of parkour has led to the opening of numerous gyms and training grounds for traceurs. Additionally, there are now several programs to certify traceurs to become teachers of the discipline. This growth in parkour-related business and coaching has made it much easier for newcomers to get involved in the discipline. Many major cities now have gyms dedicated to parkour and freerunning. Having a professional traceur show a trainee the ropes can provide an experience that can't be found by just watching videos online. Local parkour training facilities and teachers can generally be found by using a search engine like Google.

WARMING UP AND COOLING DOWN

Like most people who take part in sports, traceurs need to do warm-up activities to avoid injuries and to reduce recovery time. Light exercises that don't require more energy than the actual workout are the best. A mixture of activities, such as jogging and hiking followed by reps and then stretches is how many traceurs get ready for an intense training session.

A rep is a set of exercises. For example, a traceur may want to do three reps of ten sit-ups. After doing ten sit-ups, the traceur has done one rep. A parkour warm-up session may look like the following:

- Jog around the house three times
- Three reps of five sit-ups, push-ups, and squats
- Fifteen minutes of stretching with a focus on knee-to-chest, calf, neck, quadricep, and shoulder stretches

After the traceur has completed his or her training session, it is important to stretch again. The posttraining stretches are called cooling down. It is important for athletes to warm up and cool down before and after physical activity. The human body can be

Stretching helps to relax muscles. Engaging in physical activities such as parkour without stretching can cause serious muscular injuries.

easily injured without proper preparation for physical activities. Joint and muscle injuries are particularly a concern for traceurs. Warming up allows more blood to flow quickly throughout the body. This helps muscles and joints to become less stiff.

THE BASIC MOVES OF A TRACEUR

Professional traceurs use a variety of moves to get from point A to point B. They often have fun names, such as the double kong vault. However, all advanced parkour movements are built upon the basic movements, which include balancing and quadrupedal movement, running, vaulting, climbing, jumping, and landing.

Balancing and quadrupedal movement are the most basic moves that a beginner traceur learns in order to build up core muscles. Balancing is a great way to start because it is at the center of all parkour movements. Traceurs can practice this by standing on one foot for as long as possible and then switching to the other foot. Once balance has been mastered, the traceur's next move to practice could be the quadrupedal movement. This move is sometimes referred to as being cat-like because it mimics the way a cat balances and walks. To begin, a traceur gets on the ground and into a crawl-like position on all fours. Instead of crawling with the knees, though, this technique requires

Basic moves, such as balancing, have to be mastered before moving on to more difficult moves.

the palms on the ground and the toes to be the point of movement. Once the traceur feels comfortable with this type of movement, he or she may start by crawling on handrails.

Once traceurs have confidently grasped the concept of balancing and the quadrupedal movement, they may begin practicing running and vaulting. Running can be practiced at a local park or field. When practiced frequently, a traceur's stamina will increase and will allow him or her to run farther and longer.

Vaulting is the act of moving over an obstacle. Traceurs vault by jumping or using their hands to propel over an obstacle. When vaulting over railings, traceurs make sure that they have proper footing and are able to jump over the railing safely. When running toward the rail or obstacle, they grab the railing, fling their legs and feet to the side, and push forward. When running and vaulting are combined, it will create a fluid motion.

Climbing is another important movement in parkour. Traceurs often climb walls, trees, and other tall objects that are in their path. Climbing can help build strength in the traceur's hands and arms.

Perhaps one of the most impressive basic movements of parkour is jumping. Professional traceurs can often jump long distances and at great heights. Jumps are followed by landings. Beginner traceurs will usually land on their feet and continue to run. Experienced traceurs, however, may do rolls when they land. When traceurs have mastered the basic moves, they then can branch out into advanced moves such as front flips and backflips.

LEAVE NO TRACE

According to ParkourVisions.org, there are two basic philosophies to the concept Leave No Trace. For one, traceurs need to know their equipment and environment. That means that the traceur should make sure that all equipment is safe when practicing parkour. If practicing at a park or playground, a traceur will make sure that the equipment can withstand the weight of vaulting, climbing, and landing. Most playground equipment is not built for parkour. Traceurs will keep a close eye on the people around. Making sure that the space they use is far away from others is a good way to keep others safe.

The second element of Leave No Trace is "leave your training ground as good, or better than you found it." This means traceurs should keep the area they use clean. If something gets broken, a traceur should try to fix it. Many traceurs use shoes that won't leave marks in order to keep floors, walls, and the ground clean. Parkour is illegal in some cities, so keeping to these guidelines helps parkour gain a good reputation in the community.

Another good practice that traceurs should keep in mind that goes along with Leave No Trace is avoiding trespassing. While it may seem exciting at the time, trespassing can be a serious offense. If a place you want to practice is a government building, roof, or area that has a closed gate, it's not a good idea to enter without permission. If caught, trespassers could face consequences such as fines, suspension from school, and even jail time.

KNOWING AND RESPECTING LIMITS

When traceurs train, they must use good judgment. Attempting a dangerous move can result in serious injury if a traceur is not properly prepared for it. Videos on the Internet may make parkour look easy. A professional traceur, however, has spent years training to pull off amazing parkour moves. In this training, a traceur has to start with the basics before moving up to the big moves, such as backflips and jumping across long distances.

Traceurs also have to have respect for their environment. Many of the popular videos online show people performing parkour stunts

Having fun with parkour doesn't require taking big risks that can result in an injury or worse. Taking care of one's body means staying aware of personal limits.

in very dangerous places. In some cases, the danger is what draws people to parkour. Many of these thrill seekers, though, push themselves too far. In 2014, for example, twenty-five-year-old Carlos Lopez was practicing parkour in Portugal. A Hollywood stuntman who had been in films like *The Hunger Games*, Lopez tried to leap from his fourth-story balcony to another one across the street. Unfortunately, Lopez failed to clear the jump and lost his life.

Parkour, however, does not have to involve dangerous stunts to be fun. Traceurs should focus on what makes them happy rather than trying to show off. A traceur should have someone with him or her during training. It's important to have someone on hand to give or get help if anything goes wrong. Training with a group or having a friend or relative nearby will ensure help is nearby if needed.

GLOSSARY

agility The ability to move quickly and easily.

confidence The feeling of being certain or sure that something can be accomplished.

conservative Holding traditional values or an attitude that is unwelcoming of change.

discipline An area of study.

efficiently In a way that wastes as little energy and time as possible.

environment The surroundings or natural world that a person lives in or moves around within. A city or farm would be an example of an environment.

fluidity The ability to flow freely.

indigenous Existing in a region or area naturally.

obstacle Something that is in the way or keeps something from moving.

philosophy A particular way of thinking or belief that is followed by a person or group of people.

quadrupedal Describes walking on four feet, or in humans, walking on both the hands and the feet.

technique A way of performing a certain skill or carrying out a specific task.

traceur A person who practices parkour or freerunning.

trespass To enter another's property without permission.

underground Not embraced by the majority of society.

urban Having to do with a city or cities.

vault A leap, in particular a running jump.

viral Very popular and shared among a large number of people on the Internet.

American Parkour
219 M Street NW
Washington, DC 20001
(202) 642-1275
Website: http://www.americanparkour.com
Founded by Mark Toorock in 2005, this organization strives to promote
the awareness of parkour throughout the United States. With a strong
online community, American Parkour organizes and also promotes
local and national parkour events and classes.

The Monkey Vault
100 Symes Road
Toronto, ON M6N 3T1
Canada
(416) 760-8989
Website: http://www.themonkeyvault.com
The largest parkour and freerunning organization in Canada, the Monkey
Vault consists of professional athletes who promote the sports through
classes, educational events, and performances.

New England Parkour
(617) 615-6375
Website: http://www.neparkour.com
This web-based organization supports parkour communities in Massachu-
setts, Connecticut, Rhode Island, New Hampshire, Vermont, and Maine
through networking, education, resources, mentorship, and events.

Parkour Visions
1210 W Nickerson Street
Seattle, WA 98119
(206) 923-8864
Website: http://www.parkourvisions.org
Founded in 2007, this organization is dedicated to teaching and
spreading the discipline of parkour. The organization also

hosts classes for different age groups in Seattle, where it has a parkour gym.

Parkulture, Inc.
278 NE 60th Street
Miami, FL 33137
E-mail: contact@parkulture.com
Website: http://parkulture.com
Based in Miami, Florida, Parkulture is a parkour and freerunning organiza-
    tion that emphasizes the importance of safety while practicing parkour.
    Parkulture wants to bring parkour and freerunning to the public, support-
    ing television shows like *American Ninja Warrior*. Parkulture wants to
    grow and develop parkour into more than just a recreational sport.

Texas Parkour
8222 N Lamar Boulevard
Austin, TX 78753
(512) 394-7434
Website: http://www.texasparkour.com
This nonprofit organization strives to build a safe, supportive community of
    parkour practitioners in Texas. The forums section of the group's website
    helps organize meetups and provides educational information.

WEBSITES

Because of the changing nature of Internet links, Rosen Publishing has developed an online list of websites related to the subject of this book. This site is updated regularly. Please use this link to access the list:

http://www.rosenlinks.com/STTE/Park

FOR FURTHER READING

Cohn, Jessica. *Freerunning* (Incredibly Insane Sports). New York, NY: Gareth Stevens Publishing, 2013.

Edwardes, Dan. *The Parkour and Freerunning Handbook.* New York, NY: Harper Collins, 2009.

Foucan, Sébastien. *Free Running: The Urban Landscape Is Your Playground.* Berkeley, CA: Ulysses Press, 2009.

Gerling, Ilona, Alexander Pach, and Jan Witfeld. *The Ultimate Parkour & Freerunning Book: Discover Your Possibilities!* Aachen, Germany: Meyer & Meyer Fachverlag und Buchhandel, 2013.

Jackson, Demi. *Parkour.* New York, NY, Gareth Stevens Publishing, 2016.

Reh, Rusalka. *This Brave Balance.* Translated by Katy Derbyshire. Las Vegas, NV: AmazonCrossing, 2011.

Stewart, Brett. *Ultimate Obstacle Race Training: Crush the World's Toughest Courses.* Berkeley, CA: Ulysses Press, 2012.

Thibault, Vincent. *Parkour and the Art du déplacement: Strength, Dignity, Community.* Montréal, Québec: Baraka Books, 2013.

Van Tilburg, Christopher. *The Adrenaline Junkie's Bucket List: 100 Extreme Outdoor Adventures to Do Before You Die.* New York, NY: St. Martin's Griffin, 2013.

BIBLIOGRAPHY

Booth, Robert. "Freerunning Goes to War as Marines Take Tips from EZ, Livewire and Sticky." *Guardian*, January 12, 2008. Retrieved November 2014 (http://www.theguardian.com/uk/2008/jan/12/military.uknews4).

Carter, Kelley. "Parkour Is Growing by Leaps and Bounds." ESPN.com, June 3, 2010. Retrieved November 2014 (http://sports.espn.go.com/espn/page2/story?page=carter/100603_parkour).

El-hage, Tina. "Sébastien Foucan: Founder of Free Running." *Guardian*, July 20, 2011. Retrieved November 2014 (http://www.theguardian.com/lifeandstyle/2011/jul/20/sebastien-foucan-founder-free-running).

Foucan, Sébastien. "Biography." Official website. Retrieved November 2014 (http://www.foucan.com/biography).

Foucan, Sébastien. *Freerunning: Find Your Way.* London, England: Michael O'Mara Books, 2008.

Grima, Joseph, and Antonio Ottomanelli. "Parkour in Palestine." *Domus*, February 2013. Retrieved November 2014 (http://www.domusweb.it/en/architecture/2013/05/6/parkour_in_palestine.html).

Holloway, James. "Parkour vs. Freerunning." LiveStrong.com, October 21, 2013. Retrieved November 2014 (http://www.livestrong.com/article/538855-parkour-vs-freerunning).

Morris, Hannah. "Parkour Specialist Matt Quinlan's Face-First Plummet into Shipping Container Goes Viral." *Sydney Morning Herald*, October 24, 2014. Retrieved November 2014 (http://www.theage.com.au/world/parkour-specialist-matt-quinlans-facefirst-plummet-into-shipping-container-goes-viral-20141023-11azic.html).

NY Daily News. "Fast-Paced Parkour Offers Outlet for Women in Iran." *Daily News*, March 24, 2014. Retrieved November 2014 (http://www.nydailynews.com/life-style/health/iranian-women-embrace-parkour-article-1.1731975).

Rkaina, Sam. "Hunger Games Stunt Double and Parkour Fanatic Plunges to His Death 'Attempting to Make Veranda Jump.'" *Mirror*, October 3, 2014. Retrieved November 2014 (http://www.mirror.co.uk/news/world-news/hunger-games-stunt-double-parkour-4371299).

Sanders, Sam. "Parkour May Run, Flip, Dive and Slide Its Way into Olympics." NPR, September 11, 2014. Retrieved November 2014 (http://www.npr.org/2014/09/11/347716614/parkour-may-run-flip-dive-and-slide-its-way-into-olympics).

Snyder, William R. "Bound for Glory: Parkour Goes from Urban Oddity to Fitness Fad." *Wall Street Journal*, January 30, 2009. Retrieved November 2014 (http://www.wsj.com/articles/SB123326016593729901).

Wilkinson, Alec. "No Obstacles." *New Yorker*, April 16, 2007. Retrieved November 2014 (http://www.newyorker.com/magazine/2007/04/16/no-obstacles).

INDEX

ABOUT THE AUTHOR

Joe Greek is a writer from Tennessee. He has written books on a variety of topics, including social media, graphic design, and theatre. Having grown up in a rural region, he spent his youth running through the hills and woods in search of adventure. An avid enthusiast of sports and physical fitness, he has practiced yoga for more than a decade and obtained his black belt in karate when he was sixteen. In recent years, he has trained in basic freerunning but admits that he feels safer with his legs on the ground. He believes that regular exercise, a good diet, and a a positive outlook are the key ingredients for living a long and healthy life.

PHOTO CREDITS